Oh! My SPEAKING 3

CEDU BOOK

UNIT COMPONENTS

• KEY PATTERNS

Key words and key patterns are presented in context.
Students can role-play the conversation used in the cartoon.

• VOCABULARY

Vocabulary words can be used immediately through activities related to pattern sentences.

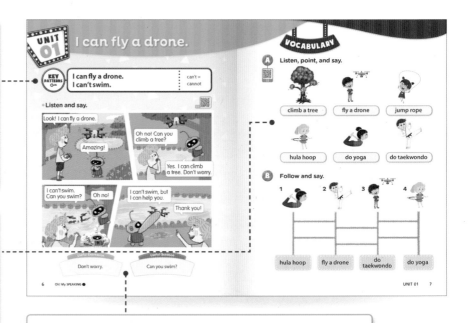

• USEFUL EXPRESSIONS & QUESTIONS

A variety of particularly useful expressions from the dialogues in the cartoons allow students to develop their speaking skills.

• KEY PATTERN PRACTICE

Repeating sentences with key patterns helps students to naturally remember what they have learned.

• LISTEN AND SPEAK

Substituting words in key patterns in a combined listening and speaking activity assists students to build their speaking fluency.

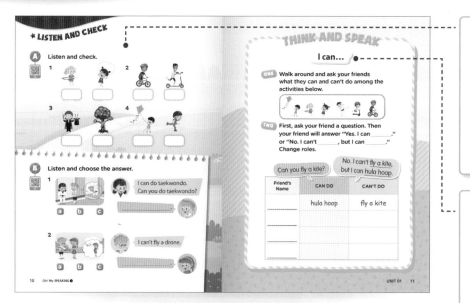

Listening practice gets students to relate the key sentences to the pictures and to learn how to use the right sentences in the conversation.

• THINK AND SPEAK

A fun and educational communication game gets students to practice key sentences repeatedly.

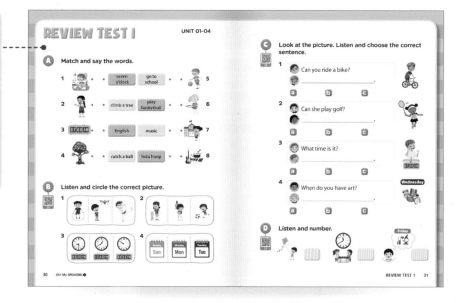

REVIEW TEST

Word reviews and a variety of speaking and listening activities help students recall and further practice key words and key patterns from previous units.

WORKBOOK

Various writing, listening, and speaking exercises allow students to review key words and key patterns learned in the Student Book.

CONTENTS

I can fly a drone.

KEY PATTERNS

I can fly a drone.
I can't swim.

can't = cannot

Listen and say.

01

Look! I can fly a drone.

Amazing!

Oh no! Can you climb a tree?

Yes. I can climb a tree. Don't worry.

I can't swim. Can you swim?

Oh no!

I can't swim, but I can help you.

Thank you!

Useful Expression

Don't worry.

Useful Question

Can you swim?

VOCABULARY

A Listen, point, and say.

climb a tree

fly a drone

jump rope

hula hoop

do yoga

do taekwondo

B Follow and say.

1

2

3

4

hula hoop

fly a drone

do taekwondo

do yoga

★ KEY PATTERN PRACTICE

A Listen and say.

Can you climb a tree?

Yes. **I** **can** climb a tree.

No. **I** **can't** climb a tree.

| climb a tree | fly a drone | jump rope | hula hoop | do yoga | do taekwondo |

B Pair up. Then practice.

Can you _____?

Can you _____?

No. I can't _____, but I can do taekwondo.

Yes. I can _____.

★ LISTEN AND SPEAK

A Listen, point, and say.

Can you _____ ?

Yes. I can _____ .

No. I can't _____ .

1 fly a kite

2 do magic tricks

3 do yo-yo tricks

4 ride a bike

5 ride a kick scooter

6 inline skate

B Listen and say.

1 Can you fly a kite?

Yes. I can _____ .

2 Can you ride a bike?

No. I can't _____ , but I can _____ .

 **YOUR TURN!** Talk about the activities or sports you can and can't do.

Can you climb a tree?

★ LISTEN AND CHECK

A Listen and check.

1

2

3

4

B Listen and choose the answer.

1

 I can do taekwondo.
Can you do taekwondo?

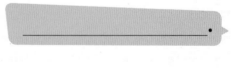

2

 I can't fly a drone.

THINK AND SPEAK

I can...

ONE Walk around and ask your friends what they can and can't do among the activities below.

TWO First, ask your friend a question. Then your friend will answer "Yes. I can _____." or "No. I can't _____, but I can _____." Change roles.

Can you fly a kite?

No. I can't fly a kite, but I can hula hoop.

Friend's Name	CAN DO	CAN'T DO
_____	hula hoop	fly a kite
_____		
_____		
_____		

He can't jump high.

KEY PATTERNS

He can **catch a ball.**
He can't **jump high.**

can't =
cannot

• Listen and say.

Jack, can you play basketball?

Yes. I can play basketball.

What can you do?
Can you jump high?

Yes. I can jump high.

Great!

There's Wacky. Can he play basketball, too?

No, because he can't jump high.

I can catch a ball.

Wow! He can catch a ball. Awesome!

Useful Expressions

There's Wacky.
No, because he can't jump high.

Useful Questions

What can you do?
Can he play basketball?

VOCABULARY

A Listen, point, and say.

| play basketball |

| play baseball |

| play soccer |

| catch a ball |

| jump high |

| throw a ball |

B Look, match, and say.

1  2  3  4

| play baseball | jump high | play basketball | catch a ball |

★ KEY PATTERN PRACTICE

A **Listen and say.**

> **Can he/she play basketball?**

Yes. | **He/She** | **can** | play basketball.

No. | **He/She** | **can't** | play basketball.

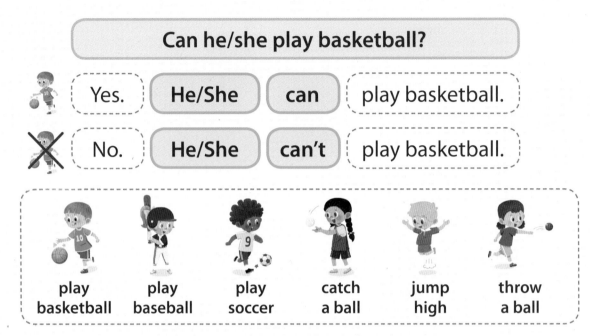

| play basketball | play baseball | play soccer | catch a ball | jump high | throw a ball |

B **Pair up. Then practice.**

1 Ken
2 Judy
3 Donna
4 Tom

There's _____.
Can _____?

No. _____ can't
_____.

There's _____.
Can _____?

Yes. _____ can
_____.

✦ LISTEN AND SPEAK

A Listen, point, and say.

Can he/she _____?

Yes. He/She can _____.

No. He/She can't _____.

1 play badminton

2 play volleyball

3 play golf

4 kick a ball

5 hit a ball

6 bounce a ball

B Listen and say.

1

Can he play golf?

Yes. He can _____.

2

Can she bounce a ball?

No. She can't _____.

YOUR TURN! Talk about the sports your friends can and can't play.

Can he play basketball?

★ LISTEN AND CHECK

A Listen and choose the answer.

13

1

ⓐ   ⓑ

2

ⓐ   ⓑ

3

ⓐ   ⓑ

B Listen and number under the right person in the picture.

14

THINK AND SPEAK

Action Guessing Game

ONE Choose one flashcard. Mime the sport to your friend.

TWO Have your friend guess what sport it is. Mime until your friend gets it right. Then take turns.

Can she jump high?

(picking up one of the action cards and then miming it)

Yes. She can jump high.

Can she throw a ball?

No. She can't throw a ball, but she can catch a ball.

Can she play basketball?

Yes. She can play basketball.

It's nine o'clock.

KEY PATTERNS

It's nine o'clock.
It's time to go to bed.

It's = It is

Listen and say.

15

It's nine o'clock.
It's time to go to bed.

Already?

Jack, it's ten thirty.

Sorry, Mom.
Good night.

It's time to get up.

What time is it?

It's six fifteen.

Let's play, Jack!

Sorry, I'm too tired.
It's time to sleep.

Useful Expressions

Already?
Sorry, Mom.

Useful Question

What time is it?

VOCABULARY

 A Listen, point, and say.

07:00 AM

08:30 AM

12:40 PM

09:50 PM

| seven o'clock | eight thirty | twelve forty | nine fifty |

| get up | go to school | eat lunch | go to bed |

B Look, match, and say.

1

2

3

 seven o'clock   get up

eight thirty   go to school

nine fifty   go to bed

4

5

6

★ KEY PATTERN PRACTICE

A Listen and say.

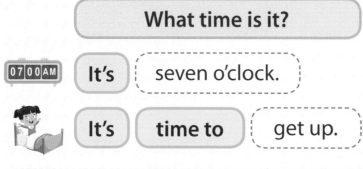

What time is it?

07 00 AM   It's   seven o'clock.

It's   time to   get up.

07 00 AM	08 30 AM	12 40 PM	09 50 PM
seven o'clock	eight thirty	twelve forty	nine fifty
get up	go to school	eat lunch	go to bed

B Pair up. Then practice.

What time is it?

It's _____.
It's time to _____.

✦ LISTEN AND SPEAK

 A **Listen, point, and say.**

  What time is it? It's _____.
It's time to _____.

1 11:15 AM
eleven fifteen · play soccer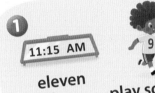

2 03:45 PM
three forty-five · do my homework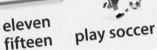

3 06:55 PM
six fifty-five · brush my teeth

 B **Listen and say.**

1
03:45 PM
What time is it?
It's _____.
It's time to _____.

2
08:50 PM
What time is it?
It's _____.
It's time to _____.

 **YOUR TURN!** Talk about your daily schedule with your friend.

It's seven o'clock. It's time to get up.

★ LISTEN AND CHECK

A Listen and match.

1 `03 45 PM` **2** `07 00 AM` **3** `12 40 PM` **4** `09 50 PM`

B Listen and number.

My Day

ONE Draw pictures of your daily activities and write what time you do them in the blanks.

TWO Talk with your friends as shown in the example.

What time is it?

It's <u>seven o'clock</u>.

It's time to <u>get up</u>.

7:00
(seven o'clock)

get up

UNIT 04
I have English on Tuesdays.

KEY PATTERNS

It's Tuesday.
I have **English** **on Tuesdays.**

It's = It is

● **Listen and say.**

What day is it today?

It's Tuesday.

Tuesday

Oh no! My English homework! I have English on Tuesdays.

Here it is.

Math + 2

English ABC

Thanks. And I have math homework on Wednesdays.

Let's do your homework tonight. I'll help you.

English ABC

Thanks. You're the best.

Useful Expressions
Here it is. / I'll help you.
You're the best.

Useful Question
What day is it today?

VOCABULARY

A Listen, point, and say.

| Monday | Tuesday | Wednesday | Thursday | Friday |

| Saturday | Sunday | English | math | art |

B Look, match, and say.

1
Tuesday   •

2
Wednesday   •

3
Monday   •

    •

    •

    •

4
•   math

5
•   art

6
•   English

★ KEY PATTERN PRACTICE

A Listen and say.

24

| What day is it today? |

 It's Monday.

| When do you have English? |

I **have** English **on** Tuesday**s**.

 Monday
 Tuesday
 Wednesday
 Thursday
 Friday

Saturday Sunday English math art

B Pair up. Then practice.

What day is it today?

❶ Tue
❷ Sat

When do you have _____?

❸ ❹  MONDAY THURSDAY

It's _____.

I have _____
on _____s.

⭐ LISTEN AND SPEAK

A Listen, point, and say.

What day is it today?

It's _____.

When do you have _____?

I have _____ on _____s.

① Monday	② Tuesday	③ Wednesday	④ Thursday	⑤ Friday
music	science	history	social studies	physical education

B Listen and say.

1

What day is it today?

It's _____.

2

When do you have math?

I have _____ on _____s.

YOUR TURN! Talk about your school timetable with your friend.

When do you have English?

★ LISTEN AND CHECK

A Listen and match.

1  **2**  **3**  **4**

Sunday
Sun

Monday
Mon

Tuesday
Tue

Friday
Fri

B Listen and number.

28   Oh! My SPEAKING ❸

THINK AND SPEAK

Weekly School Timetable

ONE Check your weekly school timetable below.

TWO Talk about your school timetable with your friend.

When do you have <u>art</u>?

I have <u>art</u> on <u>Mondays</u>.

Monday					
Tuesday					
Wednesday					
Thursday					
Friday					

REVIEW TEST 1

A Match and say the words.

1 • • seven o'clock | go to school • • 5

2 • • climb a tree | play basketball • • 6

3  • • English | music • • 7

4  • • catch a ball | hula hoop • •  8

B Listen and circle the correct picture.

1

2

3

4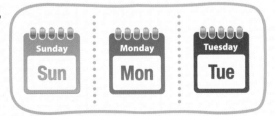

C Look at the picture. Listen and choose the correct sentence.

1

👓 Can you ride a bike?

🪖 _____.

a   b   c

2

Can she play golf?

_____.

a   b   c

3

What time is it?

_____.

a   b   c

07 50 AM

4

When do you have art?

_____.

a   b   c

Wednesday

D Listen and number.

Friday

REVIEW TEST I

E Talk about the activities you can and can't do.

STEP I Choose and write the correct sentence for each blank.

I can play baseball

I can catch a ball

I can throw a ball

I can't hit a ball

I can throw a ball.
Can you throw a ball?

Yes. _____.

Can you catch a ball?

Yes. _____.

Great! I can play baseball. Can you play baseball?

Yes. _____,
but _____.

That's okay. Let's play baseball together.

STEP 2 Draw a circle around the things you can do and an X on the things you can't do.

Activities   Sports

STEP 3 Write about the activities you can and can't do. Talk about them with your friend.

I can _____.

I can't _____.

I can play _____.

Let's play _____ together!

UNIT 05
I'm playing a computer game.

KEY PATTERNS

I'm **play**ing.
I'm **not play**ing.

I'm = I am

• **Listen and say.**

Wacky, what are you doing?

I'm playing a computer game.

Jack, are you playing a computer game, too?

No. I'm not playing a computer game. I'm reading a book.

Oh, you're reading a book! Good boy!

Yes. I'm reading a fun book.

What are you reading?

I'm reading *How to Play Computer Games*.

Useful Expression

Good boy!

Useful Question

What are you doing?

A Listen, point, and say.

playing

reading

singing

cleaning

washing

writing

B Look, match, and say.

1

2

3

4

singing

reading

writing

cleaning

★ KEY PATTERN PRACTICE

A Listen and say.

Are you playing?

  Yes. I'm play**ing.**

  No. I'm **not** play**ing.**

playing reading singing cleaning washing writing

B Pair up. Then practice.

What are you doing?
Are you _____?

Are you cleaning?

No. I'm not cleaning.
I'm _____.

Yes. I'm _____.

★ LISTEN AND SPEAK

A Listen, point, and say.

35

Are you _____?	
Yes. I'm _____.	
No. I'm not _____.	

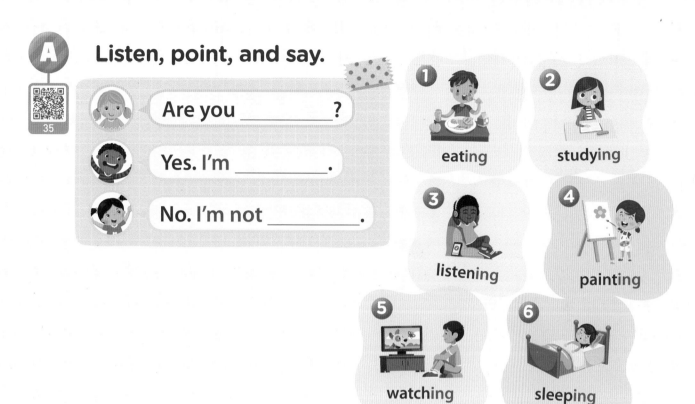

1 eating
2 studying
3 listening
4 painting
5 watching
6 sleeping

B Listen and say.

36

1

Are you _____?
Yes. I'm _____.

2

Are you _____?
Yes. I'm _____.

3

Are you listening?
No. I'm not _____.
I'm _____.

YOUR TURN! Ask and answer with your friend.

What are you doing?

★ LISTEN AND CHECK

A **Listen and check.**

1

2

3

4

B **Listen and choose the answer.**

1
 Are you playing?

   _____

2
 Are you sleeping?

   _____

What are you doing?

ONE Pair up. Pick up one of the action vocabulary flashcards.

TWO Mime and give some hints about the action until your friend gets it right. Then take turns.

What are you doing?

(picking up one card and then miming it)

Are you cleaning?

No. I'm not cleaning.
(miming)

Are you singing?

Yes. I'm singing.

UNIT 06

Is he sleeping?

Is he sleeping?
He's (not) sleeping.

He's = He is

• Listen and say.

There's Mr. Kim.

Is he sleeping?

I don't think so. He's not sleeping.

What's he doing?

He's knitting.

What's happening?

Uh-oh.

She's running away!

Oh no!

Useful Expression

I don't think so.

Useful Questions

What's he doing?
What's happening?

A Listen, point, and say.

knitting

running

jumping

cooking

talking

walking

B Follow and say.

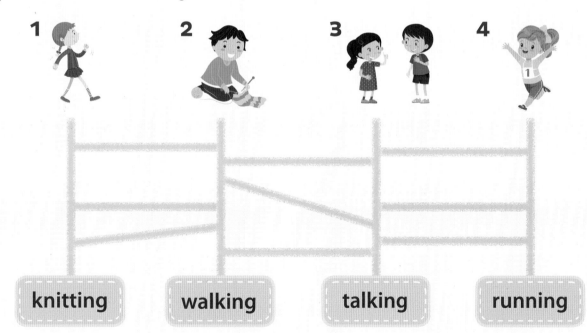

1 2 3 4

knitting   walking   talking   running

★ KEY PATTERN PRACTICE

A   Listen and say.

| Is | he/she | knitting? |

Yes. | He's/She's | knitting.

No. | He's/She's | not | knitting.

knitting   running   jumping   cooking   talking   walking

B   Pair up. Then practice.

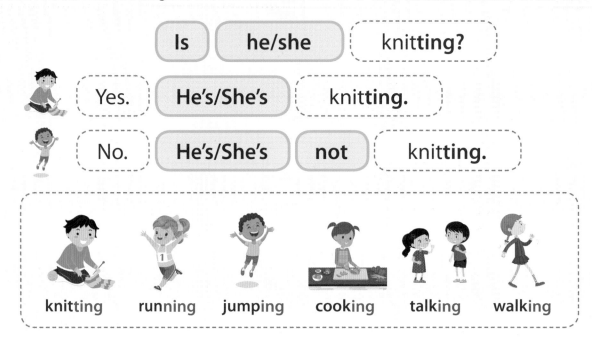

Is he _____?

Is she jumping?

Yes. He's _____.

No. She's not jumping.
She's _____.

★ LISTEN AND SPEAK

A Listen, point, and say.

42

Is he/she _____ ?

Yes. He's/She's _____ .

No. He's/She's not _____ .

① drinking

② shouting

③ drawing

④ clapping

⑤ laughing

⑥ dancing

B Listen and say.

43

1

Is he **shout**ing?

No. He's not _____ .
He's _____ .

2

Is she **danc**ing?

Yes. She's _____ .

YOUR TURN! Talk about what your friend is doing now.

Is he running?

★ LISTEN AND CHECK

A Listen and check.

1

2

3

B Listen and choose the answer.

1

 What's he doing?
Is he shouting?

a b c

2

 Is she clapping?

a b c

THINK AND SPEAK

Action Guessing Game

ONE Divide into two teams.

TWO For each team, one student holds up the drawings of a boy/girl doing an activity.

THREE One student mimes the activity in the drawing and the next student guesses by saying "He/She is -ing." Then everyone takes turns.

FOUR The team that guesses all the activities correct faster will win.

Is she walking?

No. She's not walking.

Is she running?

Yes. She's running.

UNIT 07
My favorite month is December.

KEY PATTERNS

My favorite month is December.
My birthday is in December.

Listen and say.

My favorite month is August. What's your favorite month?

My favorite month is December.

You don't like cold weather.

I know. But Christmas is in December.

When's your birthday, Wacky?

My birthday is in December.

There are many special days in December.

That's right!

Useful Expressions
I know.
That's right!

Useful Questions
What's your favorite month?
When's your birthday?

A Listen, point, and say.

 January
 February

 March
 April

 May
 June

 July
 August

 September
 October

 November
 December

Christmas

birthday

B Listen, number, and say.

 November
 March
 January

 December

★ KEY PATTERN PRACTICE

A Listen and say.

49

| My favorite month | is | January. |

| My birthday | is | in | January. |

January February March April
May June July August
September October November December

B Pair up. Then practice.

What's your favorite month?

My favorite month is _____.

When's your birthday?

My birthday is in _____.

February ❶

March ❷

June ❸

November ❹

⭐ LISTEN AND SPEAK

A **Listen, point, and say.**

What's your favorite month?

My favorite month is _____.
(month)

When's _____?
(occasion)

_____ is in _____.
(occasion)   (month)

1 January
New Year's Day

2 February
Valentine's Day

3 April
April Fool's Day

4 May
Mother's Day

5 October
Halloween

B **Listen and say.**

1

October

What's your favorite month?

My favorite month is _____.
Halloween is in _____.

2

Valentine's Day · February

When's Valentine's Day?

_____ is in _____.

YOUR TURN! Ask and answer with your friend.

What's your favorite month?

★ LISTEN AND CHECK

A Listen and check.

52

1
 January | March

2
 June | August

3
 May | September

4
 November | December

B Listen and number.

53

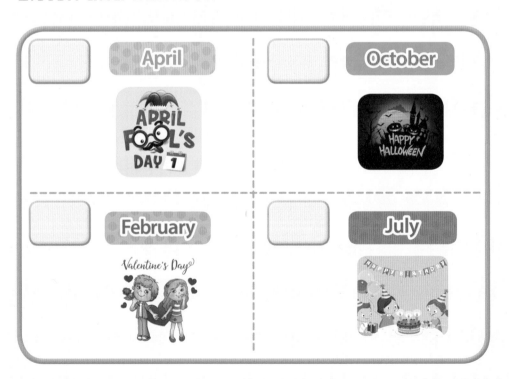

April | October

February | July

THINK AND SPEAK

Say the months in order!

ONE Divide into two teams.
Each team should cut out the month vocabulary cards from the book.

TWO The team that finishes laying the month vocabulary cards in the correct order first gets to ring the bell and wins a chance to read them out loud.

THREE If the team fails to read them correctly, the turn goes to the other team for another try.

January,... December.
My favorite month is April.
My birthday is in April.

April

Is there a table?

KEY PATTERNS

**Is there a table? / There's a table.
Are there any chairs? / There are some chairs.**

● **Listen and say.**

Is there a table?

Yes. There's a table under the tree.

Are there any chairs?

Yes. There are some chairs near the table.

Are there many people in the park?

But there are many birds here.

No. There are not many people in the park.

There are many bugs, too.
This is not good.

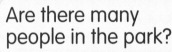

Useful Expression

This is not good.

Useful Question

Are there many people in the park?

A Listen, point, and say.

a table
tables

a bench
benches

a trash can
trash cans

a bird
birds

a bug
bugs

a tree
trees

B Look, match, and say.

1   2   3   4

a trash can   a bird   a bug   a bench

★ KEY PATTERN PRACTICE

A Listen and say.

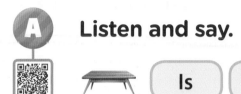

Is **there** a table**?**

Yes. **There's** a table**.**

Are **there** **any** tables**?**

Yes. **There are** **some** tables**.**

a table
tables

a bench
benches

a trash can
trash cans

a bird
birds

a bug
bugs

a tree
trees

B Pair up. Then practice.

Is there _____?

Yes. There's _____.

Are there any _____?

Yes. There are some _____.

★ LISTEN AND SPEAK

Listen, point, and say.

Is there _____?

Yes. There's _____.

Are there any _____?

Yes. There are some _____.

1 a seesaw
seesaws

2 a slide
slides

3 a merry-go-round
merry-go-rounds

4 a boat
boats

5 a duck
ducks

6 a flower
flowers

B

Listen and ask.

1
Is there _____?
Yes. There's a slide.

2
Are there any _____?
Yes. There are some flowers.

YOUR TURN! Talk about the things in the park or playground in your neighborhood.

Are there any benches in the park?

A Listen and check.

B Listen and number.

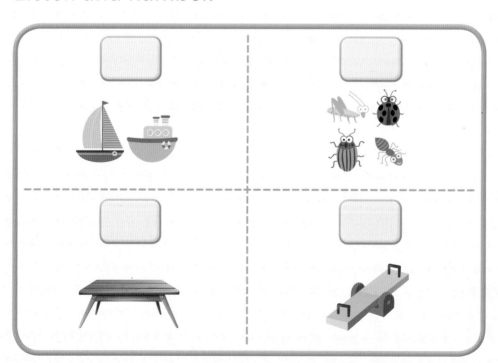

THINK AND SPEAK

Show and Tell

ONE Draw your dream park or playground.

TWO Then talk about your dream park or playground with your friends.

Is there **a seesaw**?

Yes. There's **a seesaw**.

Are there any **boats**?

Yes. There are some **boats**.

REVIEW TEST 2

A Match and say the words.

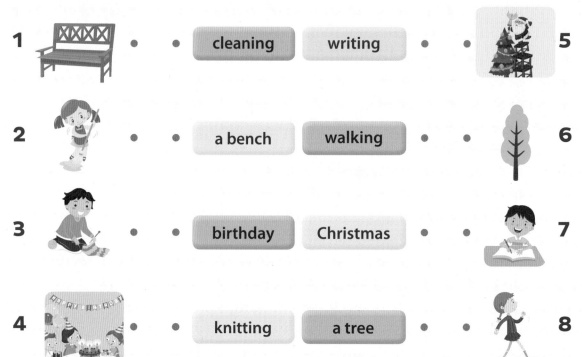

1   cleaning   writing   5

2   a bench   walking   6

3   birthday   Christmas   7

4   knitting   a tree   8

B Listen and circle the correct picture.

1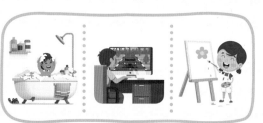

2

3   4

C Look at the picture. Listen and choose the correct sentence.

1

Are you reading?

_____.

a   b   c

2

What's she doing? Is she laughing?

_____.

a   b   c

3

What's your favorite month?

_____.

a   b   c

4

Are there any bugs?

_____.

a   b   c

D Listen and number.

February

Valentine's Day

E Talk about your favorite month.

STEP 1 Choose and write the correct words for each blank.

is in December

My birthday is in December

My favorite month is December

December

My favorite month is October. What's your favorite month?

Christmas _____.

When's your birthday?

_____.

So you love _____!

Yes. I love _____.

STEP 2 List the months in the correct order.

October   April   January   September   June   December
July   February   March   August   May   November

1   2 February   3

4 April   5   6

7   8   9

10   11   12 December

STEP 3 Write about your favorite month.
Talk about it with your friends.

January   February   April   May   October

My favorite month is _____.

_____ is in _____.

So I love _____.

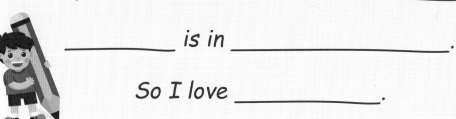

SCOPE & SEQUENCE

UNIT 01 I can fly a drone.

Key Patterns	Vocabulary	Useful Expression	Goals
I can fly a drone. I can't swim.	climb a tree / fly a drone / jump rope / hula hoop / do yoga / do taekwondo / fly a kite / do magic tricks / do yo-yo tricks / ride a bike / ride a kick scooter / inline skate	Don't worry. **Useful Question** Can you swim?	• Talking about abilities • Making affirmative/negative statements ● Theme Outdoor activities

UNIT 02 He can't jump high.

Key Patterns	Vocabulary	Useful Expressions	Goals
He can catch a ball. He can't jump high.	play basketball / play baseball / play soccer / catch a ball / jump high / throw a ball / play badminton / play volleyball / play golf / kick a ball / hit a ball / bounce a ball	There's Wacky. No, because he can't jump high. **Useful Questions** What can you do? Can he play basketball?	• Talking about a third person's abilities • Making affirmative/negative statements ● Theme Sports

UNIT 03 It's nine o'clock.

Key Patterns	Vocabulary	Useful Expressions	Goals
It's nine o'clock. It's time to go to bed.	seven o'clock / eight thirty / twelve forty / nine fifty / get up / go to school / eat lunch / go to bed / eleven fifteen / play soccer / three forty-five / do my homework / six fifty-five / brush my teeth	Already? Sorry, Mom. **Useful Question** What time is it?	• Talking about time • Making future tense statements ● Theme Time

UNIT 04 I have English on Tuesdays.

Key Patterns	Vocabulary	Useful Expressions	Goals
It's Tuesday. I have English on Tuesdays.	Monday / Tuesday / Wednesday / Thursday / Friday / Saturday / Sunday / English / math / art / music / science / history / social studies / physical education	Here it is. I'll help you. You're the best. **Useful Question** What day is it today?	• Talking about the days of the week • Talking about study subjects ● Theme Days of the week / Study subjects

REVIEW TEST 1 UNIT 01-04

UNIT 05 I'm playing a computer game.

Key Patterns	Vocabulary	Useful Expression	Goals
I'm **playing**. I'm not **playing**.	playing / reading / singing / cleaning / washing / writing / eating / studying / listening / painting / watching / sleeping	Good boy! **Useful Question** What are you doing?	• Making present continuous statements • Making affirmative/negative statements ● Theme Actions in the room

UNIT 06 Is he sleeping?

Key Patterns	Vocabulary	Useful Expression	Goals
Is he **sleeping**? He's (not) **sleeping**.	knitting / running / jumping / cooking / talking / walking / drinking / shouting / drawing / clapping / laughing / dancing	I don't think so. **Useful Questions** What's he doing? What's happening?	• Asking in present continuous tense • Making affirmative/negative statements ● Theme Actions at recess time

UNIT 07 My favorite month is December.

Key Patterns	Vocabulary	Useful Expressions	Goals
My favorite month is December. My birthday is in December.	January / February / March / April / May / June / July / August / September / October / November / December / Christmas / birthday / New Year's Day / Valentine's Day / April Fool's Day / Mother's Day / Halloween	I know. That's right! **Useful Questions** What's your favorite month? When's your birthday?	• Talking about months • Talking about special events ● Theme Months

UNIT 08 Is there a table?

Key Patterns	Vocabulary	Useful Expression	Goal
Is there **a table**? There's **a table**. Are there any **chairs**? There are some **chairs**.	a table / tables, a bench / benches, a trash can / trash cans, a bird / birds, a bug / bugs, a tree / trees, a seesaw / seesaws, a slide / slides, a merry-go-round / merry-go-rounds, a boat / boats, a duck / ducks, a flower / flowers	This is not good. **Useful Question** Are there many people in the park?	• Asking and answering using quantifiers ● Theme Fun in the park

REVIEW TEST 2 UNIT 05-08

WORD LIST

VOCABULARY FLASHCARDS

UNIT 01
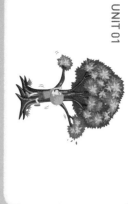

UNIT 01

UNIT 01

UNIT 02

UNIT 01

UNIT 01

UNIT 01

UNIT 02

UNIT 01

UNIT 01

UNIT 01

UNIT 02

UNIT 01

UNIT 01

UNIT 02

UNIT 02

climb a tree	fly a drone	jump rope	hula hoop
do yoga	do taekwondo	fly a kite	do magic tricks
do yo-yo tricks	ride a bike	ride a kick scooter	inline skate
play basketball	play baseball	play soccer	catch a ball

VOCABULARY FLASHCARDS

UNIT 02

UNIT 02

UNIT 02

UNIT 03

07:00 AM

UNIT 03

UNIT 02

UNIT 02

UNIT 03

08:30 AM

UNIT 03

UNIT 02

UNIT 02

UNIT 03

12:40 PM

UNIT 03

UNIT 02

UNIT 02

UNIT 03

09:50 PM

UNIT 03

jump high	play golf	seven o'clock	get up
throw a ball	kick a ball	eight thirty	go to school
play badminton	hit a ball	twelve forty	eat lunch
play volleyball	bounce a ball	nine fifty	go to bed

VOCABULARY FLASHCARDS

UNIT 03	UNIT 03	UNIT 03	UNIT 03
11:15 AM			Sunday / Sun
06:55 PM	Monday / Mon	Thursday / Thu	Wednesday / Wed

UNIT 03 — 11:15 AM

UNIT 03 — 06:55 PM

UNIT 03 —  (9)

UNIT 03 —

UNIT 03 — 03:45 PM

UNIT 03 —

UNIT 04 — Sunday / Sun

UNIT 04 — Wednesday / Wed

UNIT 04 — Thursday / Thu

UNIT 04 — Friday / Fri

UNIT 04 — Monday / Mon

UNIT 04 — Saturday / Sat

UNIT 04 — Tuesday / Tue

UNIT 04 —

UNIT 04 —

UNIT 04 —

eleven fifteen

six fifty-five

Wednesday

Sunday

play soccer

brush my teeth

Thursday

English

three forty-five

Monday

Friday

math

do my homework

Tuesday

Saturday

art

UNIT 04

UNIT 04

UNIT 05

UNIT 05

UNIT 04

UNIT 05

UNIT 05

UNIT 05

UNIT 04

UNIT 05

UNIT 05

UNIT 05

UNIT 04

UNIT 05

UNIT 05

UNIT 05

 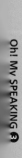

social studies	history	science	music
singing	reading	playing	physical education
eating	writing	washing	cleaning
watching	painting	listening	studying

UNIT 05

UNIT 06

UNIT 06

UNIT 06

UNIT 06

UNIT 06

UNIT 06

UNIT 06

UNIT 06

UNIT 06

UNIT 07

UNIT 07

January

UNIT 07

February

UNIT 07

March

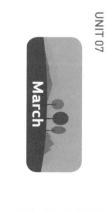

sleeping	knitting	running	jumping
cooking	talking	walking	drinking
shouting	drawing	clapping	laughing
dancing	January	February	March

VOCABULARY FLASHCARDS

UNIT 07

April

UNIT 07

May

UNIT 07

June

UNIT 07

July

UNIT 07

August

UNIT 07

September

UNIT 07

October

UNIT 07

November

UNIT 07

December

UNIT 07

UNIT 07

UNIT 07

January

UNIT 07

February

Valentine's Day

UNIT 07

April

APRIL FOOL'S DAY 1

UNIT 07

May

UNIT 07

October

HAPPY HALLOWEEN

April	August	December	Valentine's Day
May	September	Christmas	April Fool's Day
June	October	birthday	Mother's Day
July	November	New Year's Day	Halloween

UNIT 08

UNIT 08

UNIT 08

UNIT 08

UNIT 08

UNIT 08

UNIT 08

UNIT 08

UNIT 08

UNIT 08

UNIT 08

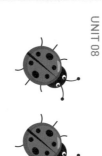

UNIT 08

UNIT 08

UNIT 08

UNIT 08

a table	a bench	a trash can	a bird
a bug	a tree	tables	benches
trash cans	birds	bugs	trees
a seesaw	a slide	a merry-go-round	a boat

UNIT 08
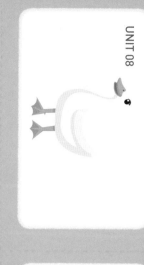

UNIT 08

UNIT 08
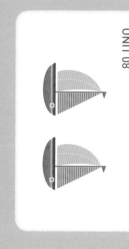

UNIT 08

UNIT 08
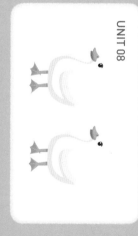

UNIT 08

UNIT 08

UNIT 08

UNIT 08

a duck

merry-go-
rounds

a flower

boats

seesaws

ducks

slides

flowers

UNIT 01

I can

UNIT 02

He can

UNIT 02

She can

UNIT 03

It's

UNIT 01

I can't

UNIT 02

He can't

UNIT 02

She can't

UNIT 03

It's time to

UNIT 04

It's _____.

UNIT 04

**I have _____
on _____ s.**

UNIT 05

I'm -ing.

UNIT 05

I'm not -ing.

UNIT 06

Is he -ing?

UNIT 06

He's -ing.

UNIT 06

He's not -ing.

UNIT 06

Is she -ing?

UNIT 06

She's -ing.

UNIT 07

My favorite month is

UNIT 08

Is there

UNIT 08

Are there any

UNIT 06

She's not -ing.

UNIT 07

My birthday is in

UNIT 08

There's

UNIT 08

There are some

with 세이펜

| 원어민 음성을
실시간 반복학습 | | 단어 및 대화의
우리말 해석 듣기 | | 선생님의 Workbook
Guide로 혼자서도 쉽게 학습 |

세이펜 핀파일 다운로드 안내

STEP 1 세이펜과 컴퓨터를 USB 케이블로 연결하세요.

STEP 2 쎄듀북 홈페이지(www.cedubook.com)에 접속 후, 학습자료실 메뉴에서 학습할 교재를 찾아 이동합니다.

> 초등교재 ▶ ELT ▶ 학습교재 클릭 ▶ 세이펜 핀파일 자료 클릭
> ▶ 다운로드 (저장을 '다른 이름으로 저장'으로 변경하여 저장소를 USB로 변경) ▶ 완료

STEP 3 음원 다운로드가 완료되면 세이펜과 컴퓨터의 USB 케이블을 분리하세요.

STEP 4 세이펜을 분리하면 "시스템을 초기화 중입니다. 잠시만 기다려 주세요." 라는 멘트가 나옵니다.

STEP 5 멘트 종료 후 세이펜을 〈Oh! My Speaking〉 표지에 대보세요.
효과음이 나온 후 바로 학습을 시작할 수 있습니다.

참고사항

◆ 세이펜은 본 교재에 포함되어 있지 않습니다. 별도로 구매하여 이용할 수 있으며, 기존에 보유하신 세이펜이 있다면 핀파일만 다운로드해서
바로 이용하실 수 있습니다.

◆ 세이펜에서 제작된 모든 기종(기존에 보유하고 계신 기종도 호환 가능)으로 사용이 가능합니다.

◆ 모든 기종은 세이펜에서 권장하는 최신 펌웨어 업데이트를 진행해 주시기 바랍니다.
업데이트는 세이펜 홈페이지(www.saypen.com)에서 가능합니다.

◆ 핀파일은 쎄듀북 홈페이지(www.cedubook.com)와 세이펜 홈페이지(www.saypen.com)에서 모두 다운로드 가능합니다.

◆ 세이펜을 이용하지 않는 학습자는 쎄듀북 홈페이지 부가학습자료, 교재 내 QR코드 이미지 등을 활용하여 원어민 음성으로 학습하실 수 있습니다.

◆ 기타 문의사항은 www.cedubook.com / 02-3272-4766으로 연락 바랍니다.

Oh! My SPEAKING

3

with SAYPEN

MP3 CD Included

CEDUBOOK

Oh! My SPEAKING 3

WORKBOOK

CEDU BOOK

I can fly a drone.

A Unscramble and trace the words.

HELP

1

l c i
b m

_____ a tree

2

k b i e

ride a _____

3

a g y o

do _____

4

l y f

_____ a drone

B Look and write.

HELP

1

I can _____ .

2

I can't ride a bike,

but I can _____ .

Trace and write.

| do taekwondo | | fly a drone |
| climb a tree | fly a kite | ride a kick scooter |

1

Can you _____ ?

Yes. I can _____ .

2

Can you _____ ?

Yes. I can _____ .

3

Can you fly a drone? _____

No. I can't _____

but I can _____ .

4

Can you _____ ?

Yes. I can _____ .

D What can you do? Listen and number.

E Listen and choose the right sentence for the blank.

1

 Can you inline skate?

 a b c

2

 I can do taekwondo.
Can you do taekwondo?

 a b c

F Choose the right answer for the blank.

HELP

a I can't swim

b I can climb a tree

c I can fly a drone

YOUR TURN! Choose the activities and complete the sentences.

I can't _____

but I can _____

UNIT 02 He can't jump high.

A Unscramble and trace the words, then match with the pictures.

HELP

1 t c a h c _____ a ball •   •

2 o b n u e c _____ a ball •   •

3 t w h o r _____ a ball •   •

4 c k k i _____ a ball •   •

B Look and write.

HELP

1 He can _____

   He can't _____

2 She can _____

   She can't _____

Trace and write.

| bounce a ball | play badminton | play basketball |
| play volleyball | throw a ball | play soccer |

1

Can he _____?

Yes. He can _____.

2

Can he play basketball?

No. He can't _____.

He can _____.

3

Can she _____?

Yes. She can _____.

4

Can she throw a ball?

No. She can't _____.

She can _____.

D. Listen and choose the right picture.

1

2

3

4

E. Listen and choose the right sentence for the blank.

1

There's Tom.
Can he play volleyball?

a b c

2

There's Donna.
Can she catch a ball?

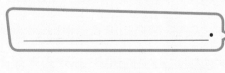

a b c

F Choose the right answer for the blank.

(HELP)

Jack, can you play basketball?

Yes. I can play basketball.

What can you do? Can you jump high?

Yes. _____.

Great!

There's Wacky. Can he play basketball, too?

No, _____ jump high.

I can catch a ball.

Wow! _____. Awesome!

a I can jump high

b He can catch a ball

c because he can't

YOUR TURN! **Ask your friend what activities he/she can and can't do. Then write.**

My friend's name:
- -

He/She can

He/She can't

UNIT 03 It's nine o'clock.

A Match and fill in the blanks.

HELP

1   • • go to s____ ____oo____

2  • • ____e____ up

3  • • ____ ____t lunch

4   • • ____o to ____ ____ ____

B What time is it? Look and write.

HELP

1   It's _____ forty.

2   It's _____ o'clock.

3  It's eight _____ .

C Trace and write.

HELP

| time | eleven fifteen three forty-five seven fifty-five nine fifty |
| activity | do my homework play soccer brush my teeth |

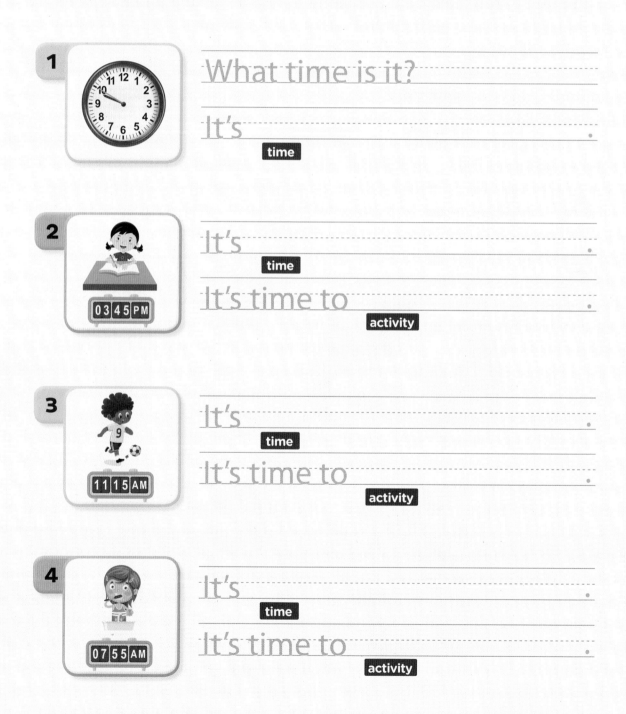

1

What time is it?

It's _____ time _____

2

It's _____ time _____

It's time to _____ activity _____

3

It's _____ time _____

It's time to _____ activity _____

4

It's _____ time _____

It's time to _____ activity _____

D Listen and choose the right picture.

1

2

3

4

E Listen and choose the right sentence for the blank.

1

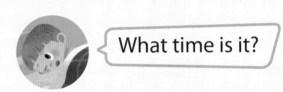

What time is it?

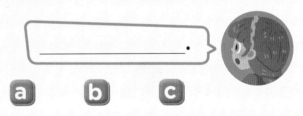

a b c

2

Sorry, Mom.
Good night.

a b c

F Choose the right answer for the blank.

HELP

a It's time to get up

b it's ten thirty

c It's time to go to bed

 **YOUR TURN!** **What time is it? What do you do at this time? Draw and write.**

It's _____
(time)

It's time to _____
(activity)

I have English on Tuesdays.

A Complete the puzzle.

HELP

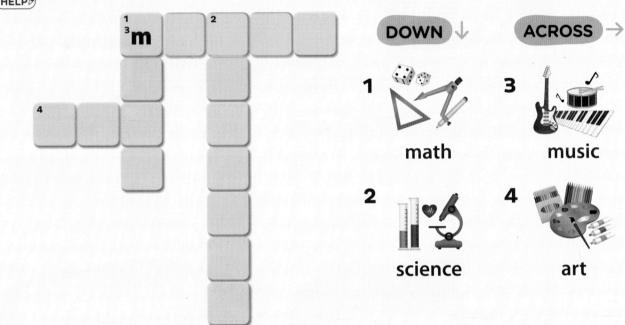

DOWN ↓

1 math

2 science

ACROSS →

3 music

4 art

B What day is it today? Look and write.

HELP

1 **Mon**   It's _____

2 **Wed**   It's _____

3 **Sat**   It's _____

C Trace and write.

| science on Tuesdays | Sunday |
| math on Wednesdays | English and art on Mondays |

1
Sun

What day is it today?

It's _____ .

2
Wed

When do you have math?

I have _____ .

3
Tue

When do you have science?

I have _____ .

4
Mon

When do you have English
and art?

I have _____
_____ .

D Listen and number.

HELP

Monday	Tuesday	Wednesday	Thursday	Friday

E Listen and choose the right sentence for the blank.

HELP

1

 What day is it today? | Sat

 a   b   c _____.

2

 When do you have English?   Thu

 a   b   c _____.

F Choose the right answer for the blank.

HELP

What day is it today?

_____

Tuesday

Oh no! My English homework!

_____

Here it is.

Math + 2 -

English ABC

Let's do your homework tonight. I'll help you.

Thanks. And _____ on Wednesdays.

Thanks. You're the best.

a It's Tuesday

b I have math homework

c I have English on Tuesdays

YOUR TURN! What do you have on Fridays? Check and write.

I have _____ on Fridays.

I'm playing a computer game.

A Unscramble the words.

HELP

1

c e l
n a
g i n

2

a s w
i n h g

3

i n a
p n
i g t

4

i l e
t s n
g i n

B Look and write.

HELP

1 I'm _____

2 I'm _____

3 I'm not _____

I'm _____

C Trace and write.

listening   painting   eating   reading   studying

1

Are you _____?

Yes. I'm _____.

2

Are you eating?

No. I'm not _____.

3

Are you _____?

Yes. I'm _____.

4

Are you listening?

No. I'm not _____.

I'm _____.

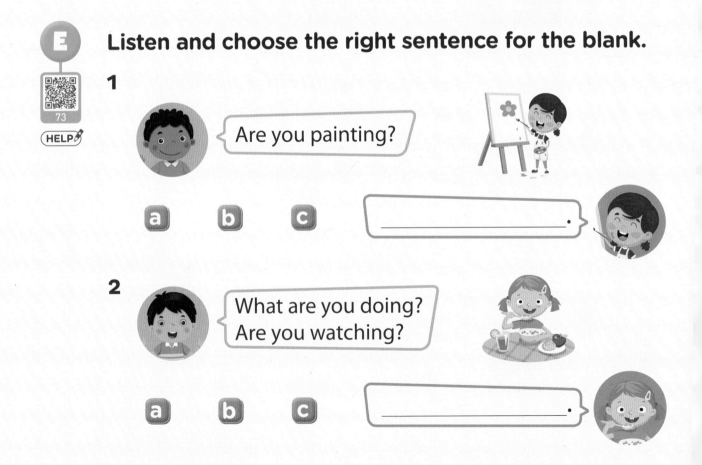

D Listen and draw O and X below the pictures.

72
HELP

1

2

3

4

E Listen and choose the right sentence for the blank.

73
HELP

1

Are you painting?

a b c

2

What are you doing?
Are you watching?

a b c

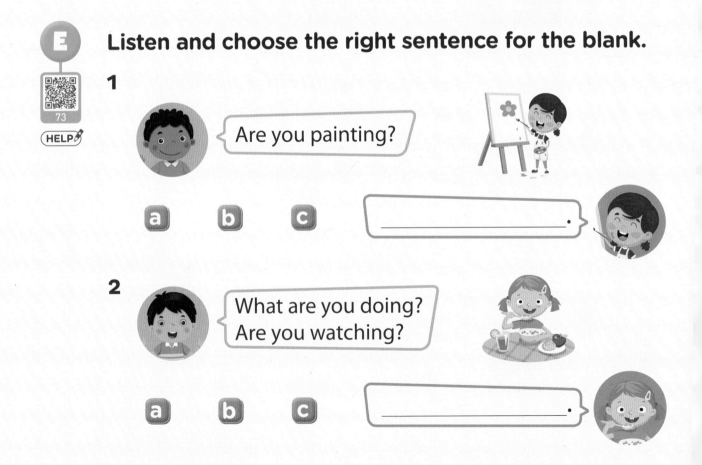

F Choose the right answer for the blank.

HELP

Wacky, what are you doing?

_____ a computer game.

Jack, are you playing a computer game, too?

No. _____ a computer game. I'm reading a book.

Oh, you're reading a book! Good boy!

Yes. _____ a fun book.

What are you reading?

I'm reading *How to Play Computer Games*.

a I'm playing

b I'm reading

c I'm not playing

 YOUR TURN! **Look at the pictures and guess. Complete the sentences.**

cleaning
washing
writing
studying

 I'm not _____ .

I'm _____ .

Is he sleeping?

A Unscramble the words and match.

(HELP)

1 o c k
   i g o n
   _____ •

2 g w k
   l a i n
   _____ •

3 a t l
   n i g k
   _____ •

4 u n i
   r n g n
   _____ •

B Look and write.

(HELP)

1

She's _____

She's not _____

2

He's _____

He's not _____

C Trace and write.

HELP

talking   dancing   clapping   jumping   shouting

1

Is he _____ ?

Yes. He's _____ .

2

Is he talking?

No. He's not _____ .

3

Is she _____ ?

Yes. She's _____ .

4

What's she doing?

Is she shouting?

No. She's not _____ ,

but she's _____ .

D Listen and number.

E Listen and choose the right sentence for the blank.

1

 What's he doing? Is he knitting?

 a   b   c

2

 Is she talking?

 a   b   c

Choose the right answer for the blank.

a She's running away   b He's not sleeping

c He's knitting

YOUR TURN! Look at your friend. What is he/she doing?
Complete the sentences.

There's _____ . He's _____ .
　　　　(name)　　　　　　　　(action)

There's _____ . She's _____ .

UNIT 07 My favorite month is December.

A Match and fill in the blanks.

(HELP✎)

1 January • • ___ u ___ e

2 November • • J a ___ u a ___ ___

3 March • • M ___ r ___ ___

4 June • • ___ o ___ ___ ___ b e r

B Look and write.

(HELP✎)

1 May My favorite month is _____.

2 August My birthday is in _____.

3 December Christmas is in _____.

C **Trace and write.**

| October | Valentine's Day | April | July | February |

1

What's your favorite month?

My favorite month is   .

2

When's your birthday?

My birthday is in   .

3

My favorite month is   .

My birthday is in   .

4

When's   ?

It's in   .

D Listen and choose the right picture.

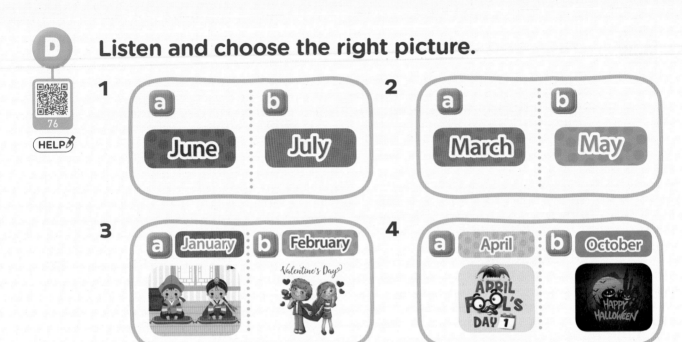

1.
   a. June
   b. July

2.
   a. March
   b. May

3.
   a. January
   b. February — Valentine's Day

4.
   a. April — APRIL FOOL'S DAY 1
   b. October — HAPPY HALLOWEEN

HELP

76

E Listen and choose the right sentence for the blank.

1. When's Mother's Day?   May

   a   b   c   _____.

2. What's your favorite month?   September

   a   b   c   _____.

HELP

77

F Choose the right answer for the blank.

a My birthday is in December **b** My favorite month is

c Christmas is in December

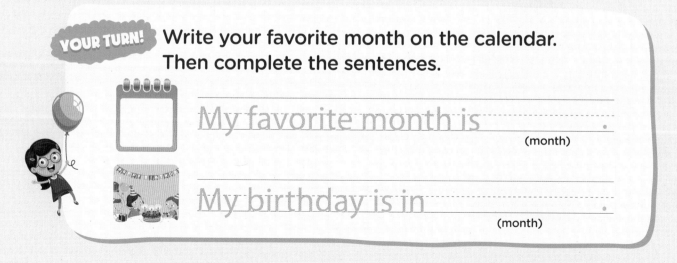

YOUR TURN! Write your favorite month on the calendar.
Then complete the sentences.

My favorite month is _____.
(month)

My birthday is in _____.
(month)

UNIT 08 Is there a table?

A **Complete the puzzle.**

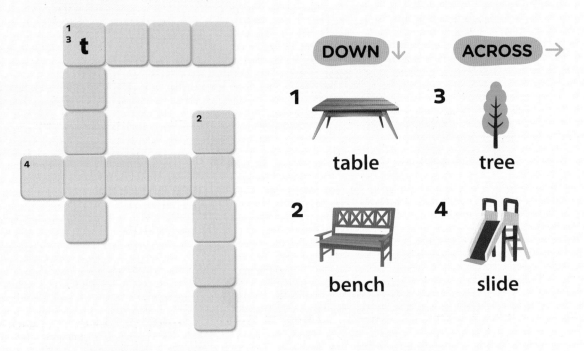

DOWN ↓

1 table

2 bench

ACROSS →

3 tree

4 slide

B **Look and write.**

HELP

1 Is there a _____?

Yes. There's a _____.

2 Are there any _____?

Yes. There are some _____.

C Trace and write.

HELP

| bugs | a merry-go-round | a seesaw | ducks |

1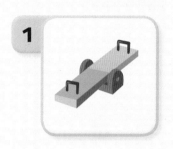

Is there _____ ?

Yes. There's _____ .

2

Are there any _____ ?

Yes. There are some _____ .

3

Is there _____ ?

Yes. There's _____ .

4

Are there any _____ ?

Yes. There are some _____ .

D Listen and number.

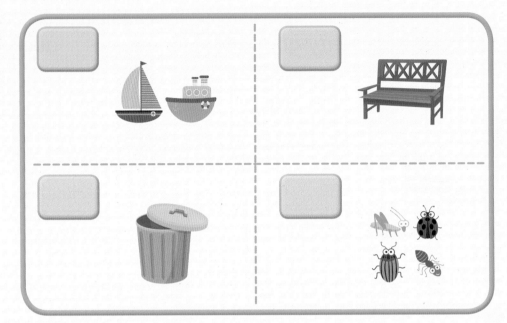

E Listen and choose the right sentence for the picture.

1

Is there a slide?

_____.

a   b   c

2

Are there any birds?

_____.

a   b   c

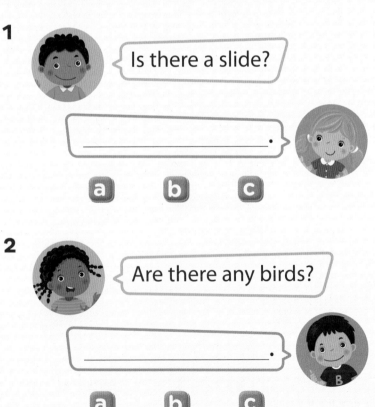

F Choose the right answer for the blank.

HELP

_____?

Yes. There's a table under the tree.

_____?

Yes. There are some chairs near the table.

But there are many birds here.

Are there many people in the park?

No. _____ in the park.

There are many bugs, too. This is not good.

a There are not many people   **b** Is there a table

c Are there any chairs

YOUR TURN! Choose and complete the sentences.

Are there any _____?

Yes. There are some _____.

WORKBOOK GUIDE

- Try to do the workbook activities on your own as much as possible.
- If you need additional help or want to hear the answers, scan the appropriate QR code below using your phone.
- You will be able to listen to the teacher's explanation immediately!

UNIT 01

A　　B　　C　　D　　E　　F

UNIT 02

A　　B　　C　　D　　E　　F

UNIT 03

A　　B　　C　　D　　E　　F

UNIT 04

A　　B　　C　　D　　E　　F

UNIT 05

A   B   C   D   E   F

UNIT 06

A   B   C   D   E   F

UNIT 07

A   B   C   D   E   F

UNIT 08

A   B   C   D   E   F

Oh! My SPEAKING

Oh! My Speaking is a six-level speaking series designed for young learners. With task-based activities and vivid illustrations, *Oh! My Speaking* allows students to build up their confidence in speaking and to communicate with their peers in fun and interesting ways. By focusing on basic key words and key patterns with *Oh! My Speaking*, students set out on the journey toward becoming strong speakers of English.

Oh! My Speaking Series

SAYCODE II
SAYPEN
Oh! My Speaking
SD4-OHMS

세이펜과 함께 배우는 Oh! My Speaking

〈Oh! My Speaking〉은 세이펜이 적용된 도서입니다. 세이펜을 가져다 대면 원어민의 생생한 영어 발음과 억양을 듣고 영어 말하기 연습을 할 수 있습니다.

*번역 기능 | 세이펜으로 책을 찍어서 원어민 음성을 들은 후, ⊤ 버튼을 짧게 누르면 우리말 해석 음원을 들을 수 있습니다.

🖊 세이펜을 대면 유닛명을 들을 수 있습니다. ⊤ 기능 지원

🖊 QR코드에 세이펜을 대면 해당 MP3파일이 재생됩니다.

🖊 세이펜을 대면 Activity의 지시문을 들을 수 있습니다. ⊤ 기능 지원

🖊 그림이나 영어 단어에 세이펜을 대면 원어민의 발음을 들을 수 있습니다. ⊤ 기능 지원

🖊 그림이나 영어 단어에 세이펜을 대면 원어민의 발음을 들을 수 있습니다. ⊤ 기능 지원

🖊 영어 문장에 세이펜을 대면 원어민의 정확한 발음과 억양을 들을 수 있습니다. ⊤ 기능 지원

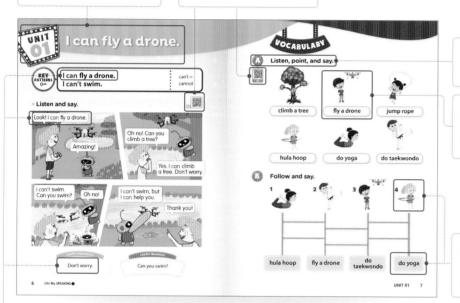

🖊 번호에 세이펜을 대면 해당 그림에 대한 Key Pattern 대화가 재생되며, 그림이나 영어 단어에 세이펜을 대면 해당하는 영어 단어를 들을 수 있습니다. ⊤ 기능 지원

🖊 영어 문장이나 단어에 세이펜을 대면 원어민의 정확한 발음과 억양을 들을 수 있습니다. ⊤ 기능 지원

🖊 그림에 세이펜을 대면 해당 그림에 대한 Key Pattern 대화를 들을 수 있습니다. ⊤ 기능 지원

🖊 문제 번호에 세이펜을 대면 해당 문제의 음원이 재생되며, 말풍선에 세이펜을 대면 해당 문장 또는 정답 영어 문장을 들을 수 있습니다. ⊤ 기능 지원

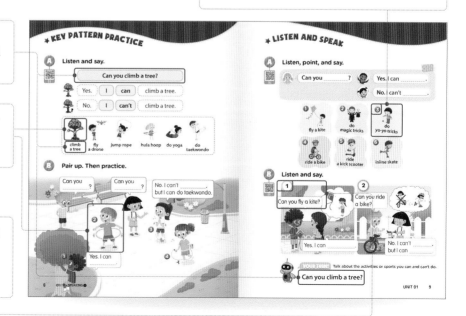

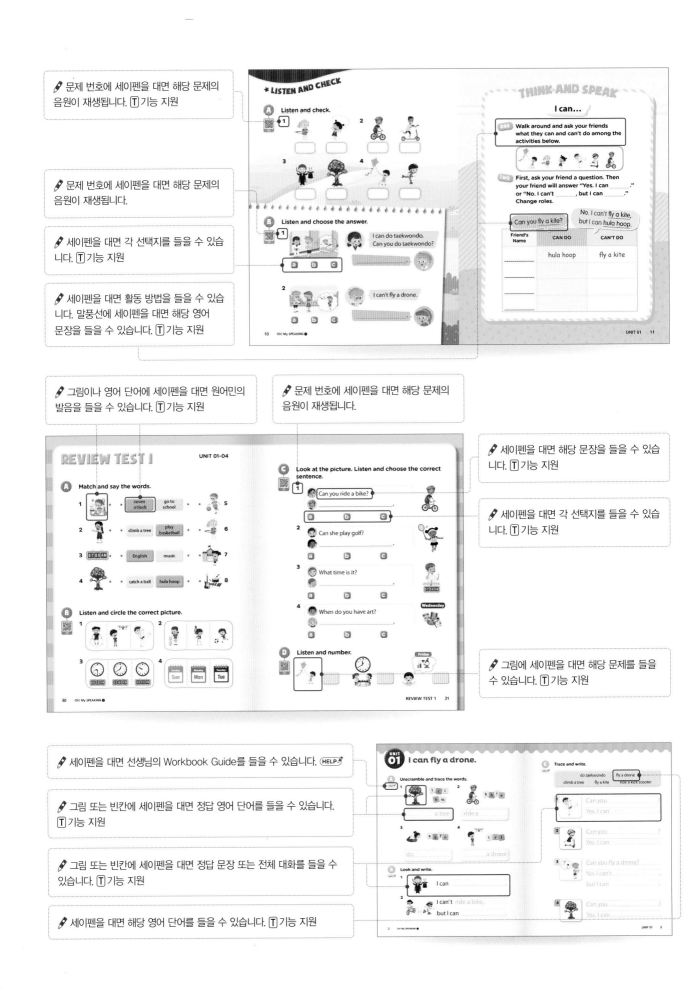